SEW
Easy as Pie

Chris Malone

©2008 Chris Malone
Published by

An Imprint of F+W Publications

700 East State Street • Iola, WI 54990-0001
715-445-2214 • 888-457-2873
www.krausebooks.com

Our toll-free number to place an order or obtain
a free catalog is (800) 258-0929.

The following registered trademark terms and companies appear in this publication:

Library of Congress Control Number: 2007928170

ISBN 13: 978-0-89689-550-8
ISBN 10: 0-89689-550-5

Designed by Rachael L. Knier
Edited by Tracy L. Conradt

Printed in China

Photo credits: Page 22 photo by Tammy Bryngelson; page 36 photo by Hazel Proudlove;
page 50 photo by Rachael Knier; page 66 photo by Trevor Allen; page 80 photo by Liv Frlis-Larsen;
page 94 photo by Tom Young; page 108 photo by Libby Chapman; page 124 photo by John Shepherd.

Acknowledgements

A giant thank you to all the talented people who helped bring this book every step of the way, from vague ideas to the handsomely printed and photographed book you are reading now. Thanks to Candy Wiza, acquisitions editor at Krause Publications, for her guidance and suggestions, and to my editor Tracy Conradt and designer Rachael Knier for all their efforts pulling everything together. I truly appreciate the opportunity to work with you. And thanks to the very talented photographers who understand the importance of clear and beautiful pictures in a "how-to" book.

Lastly, thanks to my family and friends who support me so completely and who, sometimes unwittingly, helped out as taste testers for the recipes. I owe you!

Table of Flavors

Flavors & Techniques

Introduction

How often do we hear the phrase "the kitchen is the heart of the home?" And, like many familiar clichés, it has the ring of truth. Family and friends naturally gather in the kitchen, because it feels warm and inviting.

I believe that sewing and baking are both creative outlets for our busy and demanding lives. Working with my hands to make something for my home, or to treat my family with a special dessert, is deeply satisfying for me. So, putting together a book of kitchen sewing projects and pie recipes has been a work of joy!

As you look through this book, I hope it stirs your imagination and whets your creative appetite with the unique and easy sewing designs — plus eight of my favorite pie recipes. Every flavorful chapter has some special tips for sewing and baking and, just for fun, an interesting bit of antique kitchen collectible trivia. I hope you enjoy this tasty collection of "easy-as-pie" projects.

Basic Supplies and Information

A set of fundamental supplies will be used for all the sewing projects in this book. Additionally, a little basic knowledge will make your endeavors easier and much more fun.

Basic Sewing Supplies

These basic sewing supplies are necessary for most of the sewing projects in the book:

Sewing machine

Iron and ironing board

Ruler

Shears for fabric and scissors for paper

Assortment of sewing needles and pins

Marking tools

And, if you have invested in a rotary mat, ruler and cutter, you will find these tools very helpful for quick and accurate cutting.

Fabric Specifications

Sometimes I will list a fabric amount as a "fat quarter" in the materials list. A fat quarter is an 18" x 22" cut of fabric and can often be more appropriate than a "regular" 9" x 45" quarter yard cut. Some projects require only small amounts of fabric, so when I list a "scrap", I am assuming a piece 12" square or less.

Basic Information and Tips

Use a ¼-inch seam allowance with right sides together for all the sewing projects, unless otherwise directed in the individual instructions.

When using iron-on adhesive for fused appliqué, the patterns need to be reversed so they will finish like the projects in the photos. I have already reversed the patterns in the book where necessary, so they are ready to use.

In the back of the book, you will find a section with some techniques that I used repeatedly or that just need an extra visual, so please browse through that section before starting the sewing projects. I have also included directions for the embroidery stitches used in several projects.

In each chapter I have included some sewing tips which you will find in the "stitched" block. In addition, I have added some baking tips, found in the solid lined box. Both are chosen to help you avoid sewing snafus and pie pitfalls and give you some creative alternatives as well.

Cherry

The cherry is a popular fruit and has been for thousands of years — cherry pits have even been found in several Stone Age caves in Europe! About 70 years B.C., Roman General Lucullus carried cherries with him and is said to have committed suicide when he realized that he was running out of the tasty fruit. Lucky for us, early settlers brought cherries to America and we now produce about 275-350 million pounds of tart cherries annually. Both tart and sweet cherries ripen in July but the tart cherries, also called pie cherries or sour cherries, are seldom sold fresh. They are canned or frozen shortly after harvest and available year round for baking. That means the picking, cleaning and pitting are already done for us and we can spend more time sewing. That's a plan that works for me!

To go with the cherry theme, I have selected a recipe for Almond-Crust Cherry Pie, a delicious combination of pastry and filling. For the sewing projects, I have designed two tea towels with a blanket-stitched cherry motif. Each begins with a ready-made towel and is finished off with different edgings. I have also covered a purchased photo album with more cheery fabrics and a dimensional cherry embellishment...a perfect place to store favorite recipes!

CHERRY APPLIQUÉD TEA TOWELS

FINISHED SIZE: 20" x 29"

These cheery cherry towels feature some fun reproduction fabrics used as appliqués and trims on purchased tea towels. One towel has a ruffled end topped with crisp white rickrack and the other towel has a fabric band and buttons.

Materials

Fabric:

¼ yd. red and white dot for ruffle

⅛ yd. red and white check for band

Scraps for appliqués: 4 red prints, 2 green prints and a mottled brown

Additional Supplies:

Matching sewing threads

2 yellow and white checked tea towels (about 20" x 28")

⅔ yd. white jumbo rickrack

6 white buttons, ¹³⁄₁₆" diameter

Black embroidery floss

Red embroidery floss

Iron-on adhesive

Embroidery needle

Patterns (page 134):

Towel cherries

Towel leaves

Towel stem

Cutting Instructions

From the red and white dot, cut
• (1) 3½" x 44" strip for ruffle

From the red and white check, cut
• (1) 3" x (towel width + ½")
  See Step 14

Instructions

Basic Towel (make 2)

1. Trace the set of cherry patterns onto the paper side of the iron-on adhesive two times. Leave a margin of ½" between the shapes and cut apart.

2. Follow the manufacturer's directions to iron the shapes onto the wrong side of the appliqué fabrics.

3. Cut out each shape on the traced lines and remove the paper backing.

4. Arrange a set of cherry appliqués on each towel. The bottom of the center cherry should be about 2½" up from the center bottom of the towel. Fuse in place.

5. Blanket stitch around the edges of the cherry and leaf appliqués using three strands of black embroidery floss.

6. Sew an outline stitch right against the edge of the stem appliqués using one strand of black floss.

7. Cut the hem off the appliquéd end of each towel.

Ruffled Towel

8. Fold the ruffle fabric strip in half (lengthwise), right sides facing, and sew across the short ends. Trim the corners and turn right side out.

9. Machine sew two lines of gathering stitches along the raw edges of the ruffle strip, ½" and ¼" from the edge.

10. Pull the bobbin threads from both ends until the ruffle fits the bottom edge of the towel. Knot the thread on one end only, leaving the other end free to make adjustments.

11. Pin the ruffle to the right side of the towel with the raw edges together. Adjust the ruffle if necessary to fit the towel exactly and tie off the

If you plan on using these towels a lot and not just reserving them for decoration, you might consider appliquéing the edges with a machine satin stitch for more durability.

threads. Sew with a ½" seam allowance.

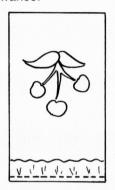

12. Flip the ruffle down and press the seam.

13. Sew the rick rack on top of the seam, folding the raw ends under ½".

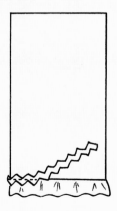

Checkered Border Towel

14. To make the band finish, measure the width of the towel. Cut a strip from the red and white check fabric 3" wide and as long as the towel measurement plus ½" for the seam allowances.

15. Fold the strip in half lengthwise, wrong sides facing, and press.

16. Open strip and press a ¼" hem on both of the short ends and along one long edge of the strip.

17. Sew the long raw edge to the bottom of the towel, right sides together.

18. Fold the band over and hand sew the folded edge to the wrong side of the towel. Slip stitch the folded short ends of the band together.

19. Space buttons evenly across the band and sew in place with red floss.

CHERRY COVERED RECIPE BOOK

FINISHED SIZE: 9½" x 8¾", CLOSED

I covered a purchased photo album with more reproduction fabrics in the same yellow, red and white color scheme for a wonderful personalized recipe book. The plastic photo sleeves are perfect to hold recipe cards. What a thoughtful wedding shower gift for a new bride!

Materials

Fabric:

⅓ yd. yellow polka dot

Scraps of red floral and red with large dot

Scraps for appliqués: red with small dot, green print and mottled brown

Additional Supplies:

Photo album, 9½" x 8¾", with clear pockets for 6" x 4" photos

21¼" x 9½" batting

Scrap of fleece

Matching sewing threads

1¼ yd. of red grosgrain ribbon, 1½" wide

1 pkg. white jumbo rickrack

3 half-ball cover buttons, 1⅛" diameter

2 white buttons, ⅝" diameter

Black embroidery floss

Iron-on adhesive

Permanent fabric adhesive

Fray preventative

Cloth measuring tape

Wire cutters

Patterns (page 134):

Recipe Book stem

Recipe Book leaf

Cutting Instructions

Note: Before cutting fabric, measure your book, as it may vary from the project model. Use a cloth tape to measure from the front edge all around to the back edge. The project model is about 20 inches around. If your book varies, simply add or subtract the difference to the pieced top, batting and lining.

From the yellow dot, cut
• (2) 7" x 9½" rectangles
• (1) 21¼" x 9½" rectangle (lining)

From the red with large polka dots, cut
• (2) 2" x 9½" strips

From the red and white floral, cut
• (1) 5¼" x 9½" strip

Instructions

1. Piece the book cover by sewing a red polka dot strip to both long sides of the red and white floral strip on the 9½ dimension; press the seams toward the center. Sew a yellow polka dot rectangle to each end on the 9½ dimension; press the seams toward the center.

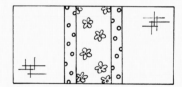

2. Trace the cherry stems onto the paper side of the iron-on adhesive.

3. Follow the manufacturer's directions to iron the shapes onto the wrong side of the brown fabric.

4. Cut the stems (brown fabric) out on the traced lines and remove the paper backing.

5. Arrange the stems on the yellow rectangle on the right hand side (which will be the front cover). Fuse in place.

6. Use one strand of black floss to embroider an outline stitch right along the edge of the appliqué.

7. Follow the manufacturer's directions to cover the half ball buttons with the red and white small polka dot fabric to make the cherries. Use wire cutters to snip off the shanks. Set the cherries aside.

8. Refer to Padded Appliqués on page 129 in the Techniques chapter. Trace the leaf pattern two times on the wrong side of the green print. Fold the fabric in half, right sides facing, and pin to the fleece with the pattern side up.

9. Sew all around each leaf on the traced lines. Cut out ⅛" from the seam. Clip the curves and trim the tip.

10. On the backside of the leaf, using a small sharp pair of scissors, make a slash through one layer of fabric only, where shown on the pattern. Turn the leaf right side out through the slash and press. Repeat to finish the second leaf.

11. Machine stitch a line through the center of each leaf as indicated on the pattern. Set the leaves aside.

12. Cut the ribbon in half. Using the yellow polka dot lining fabric (21¼ x 9½), place each ribbon across the center, right side up, so one raw edge matches the lining edge on each side (see illustration below). Baste in place.

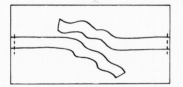

13. Place the pieced top over the lining, right sides together, and ribbons tucked inside. Pin these layers to the batting. Sew all around with batting on bottom, leaving a 5" opening along bottom edge. Trim the batting close to the seam and trim the corners. Turn the cover right side out and press flat.

14. Fold in the seam allowance on the opening and hand sew the opening closed with a small whipstitch from edge to edge.

15. Machine quilt in the ditch on the seam lines of the front cover.

16. Glue the covered-button cherries to the cover, overlapping the stem ends ¼". Apply glue to the back side of each leaf, just along the stitched center, and press to the top of the stem as shown.

17. Cut two 24" lengths of rickrack and apply fray preventative to the cut ends. Let dry.

18. Leaving 1" free, start at the bottom and glue a piece of rickrack to the cover, over the seam between the two red prints. Do not cut off excess rick rack at top. This will become your page marker ribbons. Bring the 1" end to the inside at the bottom and

glue in place. Repeat with the second piece of rickrack on the back of the cover.

19. Sew a white button to the free ends of the rickrack. Bring these ends to the inside of the book and use as bookmarks.

20. To attach the cover to the album, spread the cover out, lining side up. Place the book in the center. Apply glue down each sewn (quilted) line on the inside and press to the book. Apply another line of glue at each side edge and press to the edge of the book. Close the book and tie the ribbon ends in a bow.

The reproduction fabrics used in these designs relate so well to the Cherry motif and the bright colors are cheerful and reminiscent of an old fashioned kitchen. You can buy an assortment of repro fabrics in fat quarters or fat eights (18" x 22" and 18" x 11") and keep them on hand for appliqués and trims.

ALMOND-CRUST CHERRY PIE

This cherry pie has a flavorful filling and a wonderful complementary buttery crust. A lattice top is especially attractive when the filling is so colorful.

Ingredients

1 ¼ cup sugar

3 tablespoons cornstarch

2 (14.5 oz.) cans of pitted tart pie cherries

¼ teaspoon almond extract

¼ teaspoon red food coloring (optional)

2 tablespoons butter or margarine

Almond-Crust Pastry (see 25)

Directions

1. Make pastry first, set aside.

2. Preheat the oven to 400° F (205° C).

3. Drain the cherries and reserve ¾ cup of the juice.

3. Combine the cornstarch and half of the sugar in a saucepan and stir in the reserved cherry juice. Cook over medium heat, stirring constantly until thickened.

4. Remove from heat. Gently stir in the remaining sugar, cherries, almond extract and optional food coloring.

5. Pour the filling into the pastry lined pie pan. Dot with butter or margarine and add plain or lattice top. Sprinkle the top with additional sugar if desired.

6. Bake 45 minutes or until crust browns and filling begins to bubble. If necessary, cover edges with aluminum foil during last 15 minutes to prevent over browning. Cool pie several hours so filling will thicken before slicing.

To make lattice top, roll out your top crust flat. With a knife cut ¾" wide ribbons of dough. Basket weave the ribbons across the top of the pie (left to right, top to bottom). Pinch off excess dough at the edges, Flute the edge of dough to the bottom crust.

ALMOND-CRUST PASTRY

2 cups flour

½ cup cold butter

¼ cup shortening

¼ teaspoon salt

1 cup finely chopped almonds (sliced or slivered)

6-8 tablespoons ice water

Mix flour, salt and almonds in a large mixing bowl. With a pastry blender, cut in the butter and then the shortening until the pastry resembles coarse crumbs. Mix in the ice water, one tablespoon at a time, until dough forms a ball. Do not overmix. Divide the dough into two balls. Using a well floured surface and rolling pin, roll each ball into a circle large enough to fit into a 9-inch pie pan. Place one circle into the pie pan for the bottom crust. Use remaining dough to make a plain or lattice top.

For the flakiest, most tender pie crust, remember two things: chill the fat and liquid before adding them to the flour and do not over-handle the pastry. Using chilled fat and liquid will keep the fat solid while the pie is assembled and then the small chunks of fat will separate the layers as they melt, resulting in a wonderful flakiness. Over handling the pastry forms gluten, the elastic protein substance that makes good bread but toughens pie dough. You can also try adding a teaspoon of vinegar or lemon juice which will keep the gluten from forming a strong structure in your pastry.

You can freeze a fruit pie raw or baked. To prepare an unbaked frozen pie, do not defrost it first. Just cut steam vents in the top crust and place it in a preheated 400° F (205° C) oven and bake for about 50-60 minutes. To prepare a baked frozen pie, allow it to thaw at room temperature for an hour and then bake it at 375° F (190° C) for 30-40 minutes, until heated through. Custard or cream pies do not freeze well.

CHERRY STONER OR SEEDER

There were many types of gadgets designed to remove the pits from cherries, hopefully without squashing the fruit. The "Perfection Cherry Seeder" was advertised as the only seeder that would remove the seed and the stem at the same time, fit comfortably in the hand, and allow the housewife to perform this chore neatly and timely. This style of seeder is still available today.

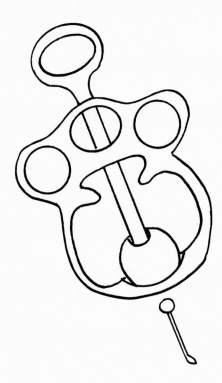

Blackberry

The blackberry is a widespread and well known shrub. It is commonly called a bramble in Europe and sometimes a caneberry in the western U.S. (and sometimes called a "weed" in the Pacific Northwest). But no matter what you call it, it is a juicy, flavorful treat with the added benefit of being low in calories and sodium and high in vitamins and fiber.

Blackberries have been consumed by humans for thousand of years; there is actual forensic evidence from the discovery of Iron Age Haraldskaer Woman, that blackberries were part of her diet 2500 years ago. Native Americans all over the North American continent have gathered blackberries. Early American settlers enjoyed them fresh with cream or used in syrups, jams, pies, cobblers, grunts, slumps, pandowdies, flummeries, wines and teas.

I selected a blackberry pie recipe that truly highlights the distinctive sweet/tart flavors of the berries with just a few spices. For the sewing projects, I chose two coordinating blue and white prints and designed a reversible table runner and a plump pillow with piping.

REVERSIBLE TABLE RUNNER

FINISHED SIZE: 12" x 38"

This is such a simple way to make a striking runner for the table — just two coordinating prints with a layer of fleece in the middle. The larger piece of dotted fabric folds up and over the smaller paisley piece to make a border with mitered corners. The reverse side is the polka dot fabric.

Materials

Fabric:

⅜ *yd. blue and white paisley*

½ *yd. blue and white polka dot*

Additional Supplies:

12" x 38" *fusible fleece*

Matching sewing threads

Cutting Instructions

From the paisley, cut
• (1) 12" x 38" rectangle

From the polka dot, cut
• (1) 17" x 43" rectangle

From the fleece, cut
• (1) 17" x 43" rectangle

Instructions

1. Follow the manufacturer's directions to fuse the fleece to the wrong side of the paisley rectangle.

2. Press a ½" hem all around the dot rectangle.

3. Place the dot fabric right-side down on your work surface.

4. Center the fused paisley rectangle on the dot piece, right-side up, so there is equal 2" margins all around. Pin or baste in place.

5. The sides of the polka dot fabric fold over the edges of the smaller paisley rectangle to form a border with mitered corners. To miter each corner, fold and press the corner of the dot fabric up and over the corner of the paisley center. Trim this fold to about 1".

6. Fold and pin each side over the edge of the center to form the miter. Use matching thread to hand sew the folded edges together. (See illustration below.) Repeat for each corner.

7. Finish by folding and pinning the side edges on the center panel. Topstitch close to the fold of the border.

For a festive holiday table, use a novelty holiday print in the center and a non-holiday print in a coordinating color for the border and back. When the holidays are over, just reverse the runner.

You can make matching napkins in the same way, using two coordinating squares of fabric, one 4 inches larger than the other and eliminating the fleece.

PILLOW WITH PIPING

FINISHED SIZE: 16" x 16"

We can always find a spot for one more cushy pillow! This one has a contrasting shirred piping trim and big covered buttons to jazz it up.

Materials

Fabric:

½ yd blue and white dot

½ yd. blue and white paisley

Additional Supplies:

Matching sewing threads

2 yd. of ⁹⁄₃₂" cable (piping) cord

16" x 16" pillow form

2 cover buttons, 1½" diameter

Extra strong thread

Long (doll-making) needle

Zipper foot for sewing machine

Cutting Instructions

From the blue and white polka dot, cut
• (2) 17" x 17" squares

From the paisley, cut
• 2"-wide bias strips (enough to seam together to make a strip 4 yards long)
• (2) 2" circles

Instructions

Note: Seams for this pillow project are ½".

1. Refer to Piping on page 130 in the Technique chapter for details and photos on preparing the piping trim. Seam the strips together until you have a strip 4 yards long.

2. Fold the fabric strip around the cord and sew close to the cord using a zipper foot. The piping trim on this pillow is shirred, so every 3-4 inches, stop with the needle in the fabric, raise the presser foot and pull on the cord to gather the fabric. Repeat this process until you have all 2 yards of the cord covered with shirred fabric.

3. Pin the piping to the pillow front, with the raw edge of the piping even with the raw edge of the pillow. Clip the fabric of the piping at the corners so it turns, being careful not to cut through the stitches.

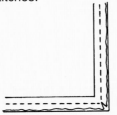

4. Begin stitching 2 inches from the end of the piping. Sew all around and stop about 2 inches from your starting point.

5. Trim off one end of the piping so it overlaps the other end by 1". Remove some of the stitching from one end of the piping, and trim the ends of the cable cord so they just meet. Fold under ½" of the fabric on the overlapping end and wrap it around the other end. Adjust the gathers as necessary and finish stitching the piping.

6. Pin the pillow back to the pillow front, right sides together, and sew all around, leaving a 12" opening along one edge. Clip the corners and turn right side out.

7. Insert the pillow form, pulling the corners of the form into the corners of the pillow cover.

8. Fold in the seam allowance on the opening and pin the folded edges together. Hand sew the opening closed with a small whipstitch from edge to edge.

9. Follow the manufacturer's directions to cover the buttons with the paisley fabric circles.

- - - - - - - - - -

There are several ways to make your pillow firmer and fuller. You can add handfuls of fiberfill stuffing to the corners of your cover or actually make the pillow cover a little smaller (½" -1") than the pillow form. You can also wrap batting around the pillow form to make it fuller.

- - - - - - - - - -

10. Thread the long needle with two strands of strong thread; knot at one end. Insert the needle at the center of the pillow on one side and go straight through to the center of the opposite side. Run the needle through the shank of one button and insert it back into the pillow center. Add the second button on the other side and pull to indent the pillow some. Pull tight. Knot and clip the thread.

Note: If your thread is not strong enough, try using four strands.

COUNTRY FRESH BLACKBERRY PIE

This pie is worth all the scratches and stained hands that are such an unavoidable part of the berry picking experience! Just a few complementary spices bring out the wonderful flavor of the freshly-picked berries.

Ingredients

Prepared pastry for double crust 9" pie

6 cups blackberries

1 ¼ cup sugar, according to tartness

½ teaspoon cinnamon

¼ teaspoon nutmeg

¼ teaspoon grated lemon peel

⅓ cup flour, according to juiciness

2 Tablespoons butter

Directions

1. Preheat oven to 375° F (190° C).

2. Combine sugar, spices and flour. Toss berries with the dry mixture.

3. Line the pie pan with pastry and add the berry mixture.

4. Dot the filling with butter before putting on the vented top crust. Seal the pie edges well. If desired, sprinkle with cinnamon sugar.

5. Bake for 50-60 minutes until golden. Let pie cool several hours so filling will set.

We have an annual Blackberry Festival in my area and after working many years in a blackberry pie booth, I can tell you that some people like their pie filling thick as jello, some like it runny and there is someone for everything in between. In addition, the juiciness of the fruit varies, so finding one formula for thickening the pies is difficult. Try a recipe and if your family likes it thicker or thinner, make a note on the card and next time simply adjust the amount of flour, cornstarch, tapioca or arrowroot (all good thickening agents for fruit filling).

If you find that the edges of your pie are over-browning before the pie is done, you can shield the edge with aluminum foil during the last 15 minutes. Just cut a piece of foil a few inches larger than the diameter of the pie pan. With scissors, cut out a circle in the center, leaving a border of foil that will cover the pie edge. This can be saved and re-used several times.

ANTIQUE BERRY PICKER

With this berry picker you will "swiftly and easily pick most all the berries located in your area" or so is the claim on the Swedish-made red metal berry picker I have in my kitchen. Moving the picker with its metal teeth up from the lower vines knocks berries off and into the bottom section. But I still get scratched!

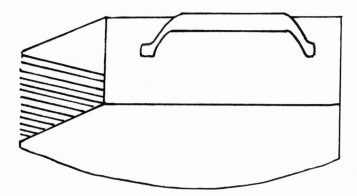

Chocolate

I think chocolate may very well be the world's most favorite flavor — there are few foods that evoke as much passion and desire. The history of chocolate goes back at least to the ancient Maya civilization in southern Mexico and Central America. The word "cacao" is in fact Mayan and the Mayans wrote about it on their pottery. Later, Columbus' son, Ferdinand, described the high value Native Americans placed on the cacao beans, which were known to be used as currency. It wasn't until the 19th century that the Swiss developed a method of making solid milk chocolate.

There is actual scientific research to explain some of the "good feelings" that result from eating chocolate. Among the 300 chemicals in chocolate, are a number of compounds that seem to produce pleasurable feelings, increase alertness and make us feel satisfied longer. So the next time you are feeling a little down, have a deadline to meet or just want to reward yourself, try a little chocolate!

Chocolate complements a lot of flavors, but one of my favorites is chocolate and peppermint. The pie in this chapter has a frozen brownie base, a layer of peppermint ice cream and a luscious chocolate sauce on top. The sewing projects are all in chocolate brown and bright pink, just like the pie. I dressed up a plain purchased place mat with simple embroidery and pink Yo-Yo flowers and added a coordinating reversible napkin and a decorated basket for the table.

YO-YO EMBELLISHED PLACE MAT AND NAPKIN SET

FINISHED SIZE: 13" x 18" PLACE MAT, 17" x 17" NAPKIN

To make unique table settings for your home without spending a lot of time, start with a ready-made place mat and add color, texture and interest with fabric Yo-Yo's, covered buttons and very simple appliqués and embroidery stitches. The reversible napkin and cute napkin holder really make it fun.

Materials (for one set)

Fabric:

½ yd. bright pink print

Fat quarter brown print

Scrap of bright green print

Additional Supplies:

13" x 18" purchased brown fabric place mat*

Scrap of fleece

Matching sewing threads

Bright green pearl cotton, size 5

7 cover buttons, ¾" diameter

30" length of brown ribbon, 1½" wide

Iron-on adhesive

White tailor's chalk pencil

Embroidery needle

Permanent fabric adhesive

Patterns (page 135):

Yo-Yo Circle

Button Circle

Vine Leaf

Vine

Padded Leaf

*The best place mat for this project is one that has 2" plain border on each end. Otherwise, use a borderless place mat.

Cutting Instructions

From the pink print, cut
- (1) 17½" x 17½" square
- (7) Yo-Yo circles

From the brown print, cut
- (1) 17½" x 17½" square
- (7) button circles

Place mat Instructions

1. Refer to Yo-Yo Flowers on page 127 in the Techniques chapter to make six Yo-Yo's from the pink fabric circles.

2. Refer to the manufacturer's directions to cover six buttons with the brown fabric circles.

3. Position the button shank inside the Yo-Yo center and sew the shank to the flower or glue it in place.

4. Trace the leaf appliqué pattern eight times onto the paper side of the iron-on adhesive, leaving a small margin between each shape.

5. Place the leaves on the wrong side of the green fabric and follow the manufacturer's directions to transfer the adhesive to the fabric.

6. Cut the leaves out on the traced lines, cutting through the paper and fabric. Remove the paper backing.

7. Use the white chalk pencil to transfer the vine pattern to one end of the place mat. Reverse the pattern for the opposite end. Place three Yo-Yo flowers along each line, one at the top, one at the bottom and one in the center. Arrange the leaf appliqués along the vine as shown in the photo. Two leaves on each side are tucked under the flower edge.

8. Remove the Yo-Yo flowers and fuse the leaf appliqués in place.

9. Thread the embroidery needle with one strand of green pearl cotton. Sew a running stitch on the chalk line for the vine and outline each leaf by stitching around it.

10. Set the Yo-Yo flowers back on the vines and tack or glue each one in place.

Napkin and Napkin Holder Instructions

1. Pin the brown and pink squares together, right sides facing, and sew all around with a ¼" seam. Leave a 4" opening along one side.

2. Trim the corners and turn right side out. Press well.

3. Fold in the seam allowance on the opening and hand sew the opening closed with a small whipstitch from edge to edge.

4. Topstitch ¼" from the edge. You can use one color on the top and the other color in the bobbin to have matching or contrasting topstitching on both sides.

5. Refer to Yo-Yo Flowers on page 127 in the Techniques Chapter to make a Yo-Yo from the remaining pink fabric circle. Cover the button with the brown fabric circle and attach it to the flower center as in the Place Mat instructions, Steps 2-3.

6. Refer to the Padded Appliqués on page 129 in the Techniques chapter to make the leaf. Trace the padded leaf pattern onto the wrong side of the green print.

7. Fold the fabric in half, right sides facing, with the traced pattern on the top and pin together with the scrap of fleece on the bottom.

8. Sew all around on the traced lines.

9. Cut out the leaf about ⅛" from the seam. Trim the tip and clip the curves.

10. Cut a slash through one layer only of the fabric. Turn right side out through this opening and press well.

11. Machine stitch vein lines as shown on the pattern, sewing through all the layers.

12. Tack or glue the leaf to the underside of the Yo-Yo flower so the slash is covered by the flower and the leaf tips extend out.

13. Measure 12" from one end of the brown ribbon. Hand gather the ribbon at this point and with the same thread, stitch the gathered section to the back of the Yo-Yo flower.

14. Cut the ends of the ribbon in a V-cut.

15. Fold the napkin so both sides show and wrap the longer end of the ribbon around the back of the napkin. Tie the ends in a bow at the side of the flower.

YO-YO BANDED BASKET

FINISHED SIZE: 1½"-WIDE FABRIC STRIP WITH 2" FLOWERS

A basket like this could be used to hold a plant or fresh flowers in a glass container set inside the basket. Or line it with one of the napkins and fill it with bread or cookies. For a buffet table, wrap silverware settings with ribbons and arrange them in the basket. It makes a cute little sewing basket too!

Materials

Fabric:

¼ yd. bright pink print

⅛ yd. bright green print

Scrap of brown print

Additional Supplies:

Matching sewing threads

Brown chipwood basket (Model is 8½" x 6" x 6½")

10 cover buttons, ¾" diameter (more or less, depending on basket size)

Permanent fabric adhesive

Patterns (page 135):

Yo-Yo Circle

Button Circle

Cutting Instructions

From the pink print, cut
• (10) Yo-Yo circles

From the brown print, cut
• (10) button circles

From the green print, cut
• (1) 3½" x (circumference of basket + 1") See Step 1.

Instructions

1. Measure around your basket where you would like the flower strip to be attached. Add 1" to this measurement for the length of the green fabric strip.

2. Fold the green strip in half lengthwise, right sides facing, and pin.

3. Sew the long edges together and across one short end, leaving the other end open for turning.

4. Trim the corners and turn the strip right side out. Press well.

5. Starting at the center back of the basket, glue the raw edge end in place and wrap the strip all around, gluing as you go. Overlap the ends in the back.

6. Refer to Yo-Yo Flowers on page 127 in the Techniques Chapter to make ten Yo-Yo's. (You may prefer more or less flowers if you basket differs much in size from the model.)

7. Refer to the manufacturer's directions to cover the buttons with the brown fabric circles.

8. Position the button shank inside each Yo-Yo center and sew or glue the buttons in place.

9. Glue the Yo-Yo flowers to the fabric band, spacing them evenly around the basket.

This set is simple to make and adaptable to almost any color scheme, season or holiday. Black and white prints with red button centers on a solid black place mat would be striking. Or think pastels for spring with the basket decked out for Easter. Even a Fall/Halloween theme would be fun. Make the Yo-Yo's with orange fabric and instead of centering the Yo-Yo hole, push it up near the top, add a stem and you have pumpkins on the vine. Paint the basket black, add a Yo-Yo pumpkin band and use it for the treats.

To make a fabric bouquet, make Yo-Yo flowers with the padded leaf. Paint bamboo skewers or small dowels green and glue a flower and leaf to the tip of each one. Use buttons or pom poms for the flower center. Arrange in a vase, basket or tin for a playful table accessory.

CHOCOLATE PEPPERMINT ICE CREAM PIE

This recipe starts with a box of brownie mix so it's easy to make and, with the rich fudge sauce on top, a real pleaser for the chocolate lovers in your family. I've used peppermint ice cream, for the flavor combination and the color, but of course you can substitute your favorite ice cream.

Ingredients

1 box brownie mix (approximately 13 oz; 8-or 9-inch pan size)

2 pints peppermint ice cream (or flavor of your choice)

Fudge Sauce (see page 52)

Whipped cream

Crushed peppermint candies

Directions

1. Grease the bottom of a 9" pie pan. Prepare the brownie mix as directed on the package. Spread mix in the prepared pie pan.

2. Bake in a preheated 350° F (175 ° C) oven just until done, about 30 minutes. Let cool completely.

3. Soften the ice cream slightly and spread it evenly onto the brownie base. Cover with clear plastic wrap. Place in the freezer until firm.

Fudge Sauce

2 cups powdered sugar

⅔ cup chocolate chips

1 cup evaporated milk

½ cup butter

1 teaspoon vanilla

Combine the powdered sugar, chips, milk and butter in a saucepan. Bring to a boil; cook 8 minutes, stirring constantly.

Remove pan from heat; stir in the vanilla. Let cool 1 hour, and then pour over the ice cream. Cover with clear plastic wrap. Freeze.

To serve, let soften slightly at room temperature. Dip a knife in hot water, dry it off with a paper towel and cut the pie in wedges. Re-dip and dry for each slice. If desired, garnish each slice with whipped cream and crushed peppermint candy.

There are several ways to use chocolate as a tasty and attractive garnish for your desserts or sweet beverages. Use a hand grater to make uniform sprinkles or melt the chocolate with a little shortening (1 square semisweet chocolate plus ½ teaspoon shortening). Let it cool slightly and then drizzle it from the tip of a spoon. Chocolate curls are impressive and can be easily make with a swivel blade vegetable peeler. Long strokes across semisweet or milk chocolate makes longer curls which can be picked up with a toothpick and set in place. Go all out with chocolate cut outs: melt semisweet chocolate and pour it onto a foil-lined cookie sheet. Cool and when almost set, use cookie cutters to cut shapes. Then cool the chocolate until it is firm and remove the cut-outs to decorate the tops of pies and cakes.

ANTIQUE CHOCOLATE MOLDS

I have a small but sentimental collection of rabbit chocolate molds given to me by my aunt. My uncle worked through the Depression by making and selling chocolate rabbits. There is a tremendous variety of mold shapes and sizes to choose from if you collect — everything from Santas and rabbits to bears, pigs, elephants, trains and cartoon characters, just to mention a few. The molds, usually tinned nickel, copper or steel, have a front and back, held together with metal clips. Many are beautifully and skillfully detailed. Most seem to come from Germany or Holland but there were American manufacturers, too. The value ranges, based on size, quality, condition and rarity.

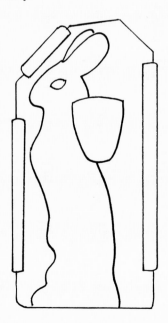

Pumpkin

Pumpkins are really members of the Cucurbita family which includes squash and cucumbers. Believed to have originated in Central America, pumpkins are now grown all over the world, on every continent except Antarctica. Native Americans used pumpkins as a staple in their diet long before the Pilgrims arrived. The Pilgrims, though, were soon using pumpkins in a wide variety of recipes and pumpkin seeds were brought back to Europe. Early settlers made their pumpkin pies by filling a hollowed out shell with milk, honey and spices and baking it. Probably tasted pretty good!

Not only have pumpkin recipes become a traditional part of our fall and Thanksgiving meals, but the pumpkin itself is a popular decorating motif for the season. So dining table accessories with pumpkin colors and motifs are doubly appropriate.

For this chapter, I selected a pumpkin pie recipe that has a delicious praline topping. For the table, I designed a pumpkin appliquéd table runner, napkins and napkin holders, all sewn from homespun plaids in warm fall colors. I used the same fabrics and a fall leaf pattern to make a wrap-around decoration for a candle.

HOMESPUN TABLE RUNNER AND NAPKIN SET

FINISHED SIZE: 14" x 41" TABLE RUNNER, 17" x 17" NAPKIN

The pumpkin appliqués on this table runner are fused in place and then decoratively embellished with simple hand stitching. The napkins are wrapped with a fabric band that has a dangle of fancy beaded trim added to the end.

Materials for Table Runner and Two Napkin Sets

Fabric:

½ yd. tan homespun plaid (add ½ yd. for every additional two napkins)

½ yd. dark orange homespun plaid (add ½ yd. for every additional two napkins)

Scraps of 3 coordinating tan/orange homespun plaids for pumpkins

Scrap of brown and green plaid fabric

Additional Supplies:

14½" x 41½" batting

Matching sewing threads

Dark brown embroidery floss

Green embroidery floss

2 (1") pieces of beaded trim

2 snap sets, size 2-3

Iron-on adhesive

Embroidery needle

Air soluble pen

Patterns (pages 136-137):

Pumpkin Left with Stem

Pumpkin Center with Stem

Pumpkin Right with Stem

Leaf

Cutting Instructions

From tan homespun plaid, cut
- (1) 14½" x 41½" rectangle for runner
- (2) 3" x 9" strips for napkin holders

From red-orange homespun plaid, cut
- (1) 14½" x 41½" rectangle for runner
- (2) 18" x 18" squares for napkins

Table Runner Instructions

1. Trace each of the three pumpkins and their stems twice and the leaf six times onto the paper side of the iron-on adhesive. Reverse the leaf for two of the appliqués. Leave a ½" margin between the shapes.

2. Cut the shapes apart, without cutting on the pattern lines.

3. Place the shapes on the wrong side of the appliqué fabrics and follow the manufacturer's directions transfer the adhesive to the fabric.

4. Cut out each shape on the traced lines, cutting through the paper and fabric. Remove the paper backing.

5. Arrange a set of three pumpkins with stems and three leaves at each short end of the tan rectangle. Refer to the pattern and photo for placement.

6. Use two strands of dark brown floss to blanket stitch around the pumpkins and stems. Use two strands of green floss to blanket stitch around the leaves.

7. Transfer the contour lines of the pumpkins to the appliqués with an air soluble pen. Use three strands of dark brown floss to sew a running stitch over the lines.

8. Transfer the tendril lines to the fabric with an air soluble pen. Use three strands of green floss to sew a running stitch over the lines.

9. Place the batting on your work surface and smooth it out with your hands. Place the red-orange rectangle right side up on top of the batting and cover it with the appliquéd top, right side down. Pin the layers together.

10. Sew all around, leaving a 5" opening along one edge for turning.

11. Clip the corners and trim the batting close to the seam. Turn the table runner right-side out.

12. Fold in the seam allowance on the opening and hand sew the opening closed with a small whipstitch from edge to edge. Press well.

13. Topstitch ¼" from the edges using a matching or contrasting color thread.

Napkin and Napkin Holder Instructions

1. Press a ¼" hem all around the red-orange plaid square.

2. Fold the hem again so it is doubled and press well.

3. Sew all around with matching thread, close to the fold.

4. For the napkin holder, fold the tan strip in half lengthwise, right sides together, and pin. Sew the long edges and across one short end, leaving the other short end open for turning.

5. Clip the corners and turn the band right side out. Press in a ¼" hem on the open end.

6. Slip the tape end of the bead trim into the opening and pin. Whipstitch the opening closed, catching the trim in the stitches.

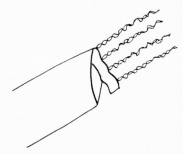

7. Open the snap and sew the female half to the end without the beads. Sew the remaining snap half 3½ inches from the beaded end on the opposite side of the band.

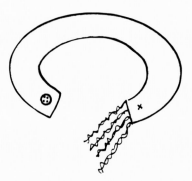

8. Close the snap and fold the beaded end down at an angle, covering the stitches from the snap application. Use a few hand stitches to tack the fold in place.

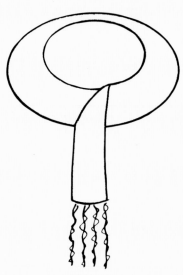

9. Fold the napkin as desired. Wrap the band around the napkin and snap in front, letting the beads hang down.

This table runner is actually reversible with a plaid side in a coordinating color. The seasonal appliqués are sewn before the runner is joined to the backing and batting so the underside of the embroidery is hidden. This idea would work for many combinations of holiday themes and novelty fabrics just by using a "neutral" fabric for the backing.

Try the same appliqué patterns on other projects: a sweatshirt or denim jacket, a pillow top, a tote bag or a banner for the front door.

These napkin holders are a perfect example of how just a tiny piece of an expensive trim can really make a difference. When you shop the trim aisles, think of all the possibilities. Maybe adding a small section to the corners of a pillow, to a curtain tie back, or to the pull cord of a lamp or ceiling fan would be just enough sparkle.

CANDLE WRAP

Candles in a home always seem welcoming. This one is wrapped with a pretty wire-edged ribbon with plaid fabric leaves and beaded wire spirals tucked around the bow. It is easy to make and removable to use on another candle. Of course, never leave a burning candle unattended!

Materials

Fabric:

Scraps of 3 coordinating tan and red-orange homespun plaids

Scrap of fleece

Additional Supplies:

Matching sewing threads

Green embroidery floss

Large candle (model is 4¾" high and 6" across)

1 yd. of green wire-edged ribbon, 1½"-wide

24" gold seed-beaded wire

Fray preventative

Air soluble pen

Wire cutters

Permanent fabric adhesive

Pattern (pages 137):

Candle Leaf

Instructions

1. Refer to Padded Appliqués on page 129 in the Technique chapter. Trace the candle leaf pattern once on the wrong side of each plaid fabric.

2. Fold each fabric scrap in half, right sides facing, with the traced pattern on top and pin to the fleece.

3. Sew all around on the pattern lines.

4. Cut out each leaf about ⅛" from the seam. Trim the tip and clip the curves.

5. Using a small sharp pair of scissors, cut a slash through one layer only of the fabric where indicated on the pattern. Apply fray preventative to the cut edges and let dry.

6. Turn the leaves right-side out through the slashed openings. Press well and slip stitch the openings closed.

7. Use the air soluble pen to draw a line down the center on the right side of each leaf from stem to top. Use three strands of green embroidery floss to sew a running stitch on the line.

8. Wrap the ribbon around the candle and tie the ends in a bow. Tie a knot at the end of each ribbon tail and cut the ends in a V-cut. Apply fray preventative to the cut ends and let dry.

9. Cut the beaded wire into one 16" length and one 8" length. As you cut the wire, remove a few beads and fold the bare wire ends down so the remaining beads do not slip off.

10. Fold the 16" length in half and gently coil each side of the wire with your fingers.

11. Glue the bent center to the back of one of the fabric leaves and then glue the leaf to the ribbon on one side of the bow.

12. Coil the 8" wire without folding it in half. Glue one end of the wire between the two remaining leaves and glue the leaves to the ribbon on the other side of the bow.

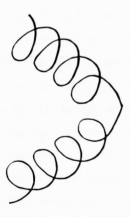

PUMPKIN PIE WITH CRUNCHY PECAN TOPPING

This recipe is for a basic pumpkin pie with an out-of-this-world pecan topping. The spices in the pie and the sweetness of the praline topping are a wonderful combination.

Ingredients

Unbaked pastry for 9" pie shell

2 eggs, slightly beaten

1 ½ cups canned pumpkin

½ teaspoon salt

1 teaspoon cinnamon

¼ teaspoon ginger

¼ teaspoon cloves

1⅔ cup (13 oz. can) evaporated milk (or light cream)

Whipped cream

Reserved pecan halves for garnish

Pecan Topping (page 68)

Directions

1. Mix ingredients in the order given.

2. Pour mixture into pie shell and bake in preheated 425° F (220° C) oven for 15 minutes. Reduce oven to 350° F (175° C) and continue baking for 45 minutes or until knife inserted near center comes out clean. Cool.

Pecan topping:

1 cup coarsely chopped pecans

⅔ cup firmly packed brown sugar

3 Tablespoons butter, melted

Mix pecans and brown sugar in a small bowl. Drizzle with butter and stir until mixture is uniformly moistened. Sprinkle mixture over completely cooled pie. Broil about 5 inches from the heat for 1-2 minutes or until bubbly. Cool. Serve pie slices with whipped cream and pecan half.

To avoid a soggy crust, brush a little egg white on the bottom of the crust before adding the filling.

To make a festive garnish for your pies, roll out your pastry scraps and use a mini cookie cutter to cut out shapes such as leaves, stars, apples or pumpkins. Lightly brush the shapes with water, sprinkle on sugar (or cinnamon sugar) and bake at 350° F (175° C) on a cookie sheet until golden. Spoon whipped cream on the pie slice and top with a pie crust cookie.

ANTIQUE PASTRY JAGGER

A jagger is a pastry cutter used to cut or trim off the pie crust dough that hangs over the edge of the pie pan or to cut shapes or strips for a lattice top. Old jaggers can be found made from brass, copper, iron, porcelain, steel and even scrimshaw (carved whalebone). In fact, back in the clipper era, sailors brought home wonderful pie jaggers that they had carved out of bone. Many of these were very intricate with figures carved on the handle and multiple wheels.

Some jaggers are made with separate "crimpers" to seal and corrugate the top and bottom crust along the edge. Some have fork-like "pricklers" for making holes in the top crust for releasing steam. And, some are made with a "pastry stamp" at the other end, like a cookie cutter, to cut out leaf shapes to garnish the pies.

Cranberry

Also known as the "wonder berry," the cranberry is valued for its flavor, nutritional content and its versatility. It is used for juices and sauces, added to desserts, salads, breads and poultry stuffing and when dried, it becomes a sweet, mother-approved snack. If that isn't useful enough, it can be strung for garlands and other colorful holiday decorations. The cranberry also has the distinction of being one of only three major fruits native to North America. (The other two are the blueberry and Concord grape.)

The cranberry is a unique fruit, and is farmed and harvested in a very unusual way. Cranberries grow on a low-lying vine; the sprouting runners grow up to 6 feet long. To harvest the berries, the farmers flood the beds, causing the vines to rise. Clad in high waders, farmers then walk through the bogs and loosen the fruit from the vines. The berries form a beautiful floating red carpet as they move along to a waiting truck. My home state of Oregon is one of the major cranberry producing areas in America. The fall harvest is a time to celebrate with festivals and parades.

For this chapter, I selected a cranberry cream cheese pie, made with a can of whole-berry cranberry sauce. To carry a pie (or hide it until dinner), I designed a padded carrier and made it with two coordinating cranberry and cream colored fabrics. Using the same fabrics, I made a simple cover to wrap around a tall ice cream container for the table, or coffee can for a stylish tool holder for the kitchen.

PADDED FABRIC PIE CARRIER

FINISHED SIZE: 26" x 24" (OPEN) WILL HOLD A 9" PIE

This pie cover and carrier is sewn with a layer of fleece to make it stronger and help retain heat. The contrasting striped piping and covered buttons give a practical piece a snappy style.

Materials

Fabric:

¾ yd. cranberry and cream plaid, home dec weight

½ yd. cranberry and cream stripe, home dec weight

Additional Supplies:

½ yd. fusible fleece

Matching sewing threads

44" piece of cable (piping) cord, ⁵⁄₃₂" diameter

2 snap sets, size 10

2 cover buttons, 1½" diameter

Zipper foot for sewing machine

Patterns (page 140):

Wide Curve

Narrow Curve

Cutting Instructions

From the plaid fabric, cut
- (2) 10½" x 24½" rectangles (center section of carrier)
- (4) 4½" x 8½" rectangles (carrier straps)

From the striped fabric, cut
- (2) 1⅝" x 22" strips on the bias
- (2) 2½" circles

From the fusible fleece, cut
- (1) 10" x 24" rectangle
- (2) 4" x 8" rectangles

Instructions

1. Use the wide curved end pattern to round off the corners on the large plaid rectangles and the fleece. Use the narrow pattern to round off the corners of the smaller rectangles and fleece on one end only.

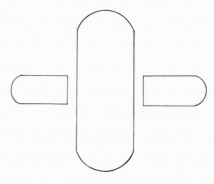

2. Follow the manufacturer's directions to fuse the fleece pieces to the wrong side of one wide rectangle and two of the smaller rectangles. Center the fleece so it does not cover the seam allowance on each piece.

3. Refer to Piping on page 132 in the Technique chapter for details on preparing piping trim. Do not use "gathering" method. Cut the cable cord in half to make two 22" lengths. Fold one bias strip around a cord and sew close to the cord using a zipper foot on your sewing machine. Repeat with the second cord and bias strip.

4. Trim the flat side of the piping to ¼" from the seam line on both pieces.

5. Apply piping trim to each carrier strap (small rounded edges). Pin and baste the trim to the right side of a fused strap with the flat edge of the piping even with the raw edge of the fabric. Leave the short straight ends free of trim. Clip the piping on the curves, being careful not to cut through the stitching.

6. Pin the two remaining strap pieces to the two fused pieces, right sides together, and sew all around, leaving open at the bottom. Clip the curves and turn right-side out. Press well.

7. Place the fused center section (large rectangle) on your work surface, right side up. Position a strap at the center on each side, matching the raw edges. Baste in place.

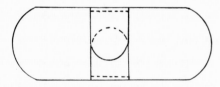

8. Place the remaining plaid rectangle over the center section, right sides together, and pin. Sew all around, leaving a 5" opening along one side. Clip the curves and turn right-side out. Press well.

9. Fold in the seam allowance on the opening and hand sew the opening closed with a small whipstitch from edge to edge.

10. Topstitch all around the center section ¼" from the edge.

11. Sew a snap set to the ends of the center section, one half on the outside and the other half on the lining side so the ends overlap and snap together.

12. Sew a snap set to the ends of the straps, one half on the outside and the other half on the lining side, so the ends overlap and snap together.

13. Follow the manufacturer's directions to cover the buttons with the striped fabric circles.

14. Sew a button to the overlapping top half of the center section and the straps, covering the stitches holding the snaps.

FABRIC COVERED KITCHEN TOOL HOLDER

FINISHED SIZE: 6½" HIGH

You can keep kitchen tools handy and in reach by making this decorative holder that can sit on the counter. More contrasting piping and covered buttons embellish the fabric wrap that disguises an ordinary coffee can.

Materials

Fabric:

⅓ yard cranberry and cream stripe, home décor weight

½ yard cranberry cream plaid, home décor weight

Additional Supplies:

Fusible fleece

Matching sewing threads

48" length of cable (piping) cord, ⁵⁄₃₂" diameter

2 snap sets, size 10

2 cover buttons, 1½" diameter

Coffee can (26 oz.) or similar container (Model is 6½" tall and 16" around. Oatmeal box, tin, or straight-sided vase could be substituted for coffee can.)

Zipper foot for sewing machine

Pattern (page 140):

Narrow Curve End

Cutting Instruction

From the striped fabric, cut
• (2) 7" x 19" rectangles (height + ½" x circumference + 3") See Step 2.

From the plaid fabric, cut
• (2) 1⅝" x 25" strips on the bias
• (2) 2½" circles

From the fusible fleece, cut
• (1) 6½" x 18½" rectangles

Instructions

1. Use the pattern to round off the two corners on one end of the striped rectangles and one end of the fleece.

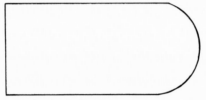

2. Measure your container for height and circumference. If it differs from the model, adjust the cutting measurement for the striped rectangle and fleece. The cutting measurement should be the container height plus ½" seam allowance by the container circumference plus 3" for overlap.

3. Follow the manufacturer's directions to fuse the fleece to the wrong side of one fabric piece, centering the fleece so the seam allowance is not covered.

4. Refer to Piping on page 130 in the Technique Chapter for details on preparing piping trim, without gathering. Seam the two strips and wrap the fabric around the cord. Sew close to the cord using a zipper foot on the sewing machine.

5. Trim the flat side of the piping to ¼" from the seam line.

6. Pin and baste the piping trim to the long edges and the rounded end of the fused rectangle on the right side. Clip the piping on the curves, being careful not to cut through the stitching.

7. Pin the two fabric rectangles together, right sides facing, and sew all around, leaving a 4" opening on the straight end. Trim the corners and clip the curves. Turn right-side out through the opening and press well.

8. Fold in the seam allowance on the opening and hand sew the opening closed with a small whipstitch from edge to edge.

9. Wrap the band around the can snugly, with the rounded end overlapping the straight end. Use two pins to mark the ends 2" from the top and 2" from the bottom. Sew a snap set to each spot.

10. Refer to the manufacturer's directions to cover the buttons with the plaid fabric circles.

11. Sew the buttons to the right side of the overlapping end, covering the stitches holding the snaps.

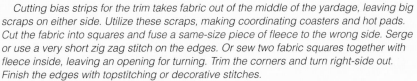

Cutting bias strips for the trim takes fabric out of the middle of the yardage, leaving big scraps on either side. Utilize these scraps, making coordinating coasters and hot pads. Cut the fabric into squares and fuse a same-size piece of fleece to the wrong side. Serge or use a very short zig zag stitch on the edges. Or sew two fabric squares together with fleece inside, leaving an opening for turning. Trim the corners and turn right-side out. Finish the edges with topstitching or decorative stitches.

Not exactly a sewing tip, but fresh cranberries can be a festive craft ingredient, particularly during the holidays. Thread a thin sewing needle with waxed dental floss, make a knot, and string cranberries one at a time by piercing through the center with the needle. You can alternate with fresh popped popcorn, beads, whole cinnamon sticks or other ingredients. Continue until you have the desired garland length. If using the garland indoors, you can prolong its use by spraying it with shellac. If using it outdoors, do not use the shellac for the safety of the birds that will be attracted to the berries.

CRANBERRY CREAM CHEESE PIE

The tartness of the cranberries and the sweetness of the cream cheese make a memorable combination of flavors in this attractive pie. There is also contrast in the nutty texture of the topping and the smooth filling. And best of all, this pie is quick and easy to prepare, and looks as good as it tastes.

Ingredients

Unbaked 9" pie crust

1 (8 oz.) pkg. of cream cheese, softened

1 (14 oz.) can of sweetened condensed milk

¼ cup lemon juice

3 tablespoons light brown sugar, divided

2 tablespoons cornstarch

1 (16 oz.) can of whole berry cranberry sauce

¼ cup butter, chilled and diced

⅓ cup flour

¾ cup chopped walnuts

Directions

1. Preheat the oven to 425° F (220° C).

2. Bake the pie shell 8 minutes and remove it from the oven. Reduce the oven temperature to 375° F (190° C).

3. In a large bowl, beat the cream cheese until fluffy. Mix in sweetened condensed milk until the mixture is smooth; stir in the lemon juice. Pour the prepared filling into the prepared pastry shell.

4. In a small bowl, mix 1 tablespoon light brown sugar with the cornstarch. Stir in the cranberry sauce and spoon the mixture over the cream cheese layer.

5. In a medium bowl, mix the butter, flour and 2 tablespoons brown sugar until crumbly. Add the walnuts and sprinkle the topping evenly over the cranberry layer.

6. Bake 45 minutes in the 375° F (190° C) oven or until lightly browned. Cool on a rack and chill overnight for the best flavor.

Crumb crusts are a quick and easy alternative to pastry and add flavor and texture to a pie. Though some recipes call for an unbaked crumb crust, I prefer to always bake mine. It holds together better, cuts cleaner and is less likely to be soggy. Bake at 350° F (175° C) for 8-10 minutes and it is cool before filling. Cookies to consider for crumb crusts include chocolate wafers, graham crackers, gingersnaps, macaroons and vanilla wafers and you can also add ¼ to ⅓ cup chopped nuts to the crumbs.

ANTIQUE PIE BIRDS

Pie birds are a type of pie vent. It is a decorative way to release the steam formed by the baking pie. They are ceramic shapes with a hole that sits above the crust and although many are in the shape of birds (especially blackbirds, probably related to the nursery rhyme "four and twenty blackbirds baked in a pie",) they actually have been made in many other shapes. Fish, owls, clowns, dragons, pelicans, Santas and cartoon figures are among the various pie birds collected around the world.

New pie birds are sometimes found in gift and specialty cooking catalogs. Not a necessity since we usually cut vent holes in the crust. They are more for fun and decoration!

Apple

Apples are one of the most familiar and identifiable fruits in the world — there are about 7,500 different varieties. Apples were the favorite fruit of ancient Greeks and Romans, but archeologists have found evidence that humans were enjoying apples since at least 6500 B.C. The Pilgrims planted the first American apple trees in the Massachusetts Bay Colony and they called the apples "winter bananas". Today, Americans eat an average of 65 fresh apples every year.

Yes, there really was a "Johnny Appleseed!" His real name was John Chapman and he was born in Massachusetts in 1774. He started his westward journey about 1797. Moving ahead of the pioneers, he supplied seeds and seedlings, and started many nurseries throughout the Midwest. Spreading the trees was important to the early settlers. Apples were such a staple of their diet and transportation was so unreliable.

PIECED APPLE QUILT BLOCK TOWEL HOLDER

FINISHED SIZE: 7" x 7" APPLE BLOCK

This apple patchwork block is an adaptation of a traditional quilt block called, snowball. Adding apple-red fabric, a stem and leaf transforms the snowball into a plump red apple. The towel hanger is actually a purse handle found in the notions department. The towel is dressed up just a bit with simple hand stitching.

Materials

Fabric:

Fat quarter of black and white dot

Scraps of red, brown and green prints

Additional Supplies:

Scrap of fleece

7½" x 7½" batting

Matching sewing threads

Black pearl cotton, size 5

Black U-shaped purse handle, 5¾" x 4¼"

2 white buttons, ¾" diameter

2 black (¾") eyes from hook and eye closures

Red dish towel

Iron-on adhesive, ultra hold

Tailor's chalk

Patterns (page 140):

Leaf

Stem

Cutting Instructions

From the black and white dot, cut
- (4) 1½" x 1½" squares
- (2) 2¼" x 4" strips
- (2) 2¼" x 7½" strips
- (1) 7½" x 7½" square
- (2) 1¼" x 3¾" strips

From the red fabric, cut
- (1) 4" x 4" square

87

Instructions

1. Refer to the section on Adding Triangles to Squares on page 131 in the Techniques chapter for detailed photos and instructions to make the apple block. Draw a stitching line on the wrong side of each black and white 1½" square, diagonally from corner to corner with tailor's chalk. Pin a square to each corner of the red square and sew on the lines as shown. Trim the seams to ¼". Fold the triangle back and press.

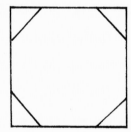

2. Trace the stem pattern onto the paper side of the iron-on adhesive. Cut out, leaving a ¼" margin around the pattern.

3. Place the shape on the wrong side of the brown fabric. Refer to the manufacturer's directions to transfer the adhesive to the fabric.

4. Cut out on the traced line, cutting through the fabric and paper. Remove the paper backing.

5. Place the stem on the right side of one of the 4" black and white border strips, centered on one long edge. Fuse in place.

6. Sew the stem appliquéd border strip to the top of the apple square, so the stem appears to be attached to the apple. Sew the remaining 4" strip to the bottom of the apple square. Press the seams outward.

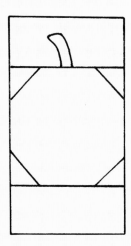

7. Sew the 7½" border strips to the sides of the apple; press the seams outward.

8. To make the fabric hangers for the plastic purse handle, fold each 3¾" long strip in half lengthwise, right sides together, and sew the long edge and across one short end. Trim the corners and turn right-side out through the open end. Press well.

9. Place the purse handle next to the bottom of the apple block and mark where the handle will attach.

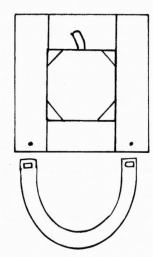

10. Place a hanging tab on each mark with the open end even with the raw edge of the bottom of the block. Baste in place.

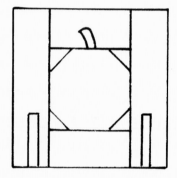

11. Place the pieced apple top right sides together with the 7½" x 7½" black and white square and pin the layers to the batting. Sew all around, leaving a 3" opening along one side for turning.

12. Trim the batting close to the seam and trim the corners. Turn the block right side out through the opening and press well.

13. Fold in the seam allowance on the opening and hand sew the opening closed with a small whipstitch from edge to edge.

14. Machine quilt around the apple and stem (in the ditch) with black thread, or quilt as desired.

15. Refer to Padded Appliqués on page 129 in the Technique chapter. Trace the leaf onto the wrong side of the green fabric. Fold the fabric in half, right sides facing, and pin to the fleece.

16. Sew all around on the traced lines.

17. Cut the leaf out about ⅛" from the seam. Trim the tip and clip the curves.

18. Using a small, sharp pair of scissors, cut a slash through one layer only of the fabric. Turn the leaf right-side out through this opening; press well. Slip stitch the opening closed.

19. Position the leaf on the apple near the stem as shown in the photo. Machine stitch through the center of the leaf with green thread to attach it to the block.

20. Slip the hanging tabs through the holes in the purse handle and bring the tab ends to the back of the apple block. Sew a white button to the front, catching the tab ends in the back.

21. Sew an eye to each top back corner of the block for hangers.

22. Use one strand of black pearl cotton embroidery floss to sew a running stitch along the hem of the dish towel.

23. Slip the towel through the hanging black handle.

APPLE QUILT BLOCK POTHOLDER

FINISHED SIZE: 8" x 8"

The same pieced apple block is made into a potholder by adding a bright red border and using a heat resistant batting. Hanging on a wall, it becomes a colorful kitchen decoration.

Materials

Fabric:

  Fat quarter red print

  Scrap of black and white dot

  Scrap of brown print and green print

Additional Supplies:

  Scrap of fleece

  8½" x 8½" insulated batting

  8½" x 8½" cotton batting

  Matching sewing threads

  1" plastic ring for hanger

  Iron-on adhesive, ultra hold

Patterns (page 140):

  Leaf

  Stem

Cutting Instructions

From the red fabric, cut
- (1) 4" x 4" square
- (2) 1" x 7½" strips
- (2) 1" x 8½" strips
- (1) 8½" x 8½" square

From the black and white dot, cut
- (4) 1½" x 1½" squares
- (2) 2½" x 4" strips
- (2) 2¼" x 7½" strips

Instructions

1. Construct the basic apple block just as described in the Pieced Apple Quilt Block Towel Holder instructions, Steps 1 through 7.

2. Sew the 7½" long red strips to the top and bottom of the block; press the seams outward.

3. Sew the 8½" long red strips to the sides of the block; press the seams outward.

4. Follow the Towel Holder instructions, Steps 11 through 19, using the red square and both the insulated batting and cotton batting.

5. Sew the plastic ring to the back of the potholder in the top center or at a corner for a hanger.

When finishing a padded project by sewing around the edges and turning, use the same fabric for the backing as you used on your outer border. That way, the backing won't be noticeable if it shows along the edge.

When tracing around patterns on fabric or drawing diagonal lines on fabric squares, it is good to use a nonslip surface so the fabric doesn't pull when you move the pencil. You can buy boards made just for this use, or you can make your own by gluing fine-grit sandpaper to a piece of heavy cardboard.

Pressing is an important step in any sewing project and especially when making patchwork blocks. Press after each seam, first in the closed position to set the stitches and then carefully press the seam open or to one side per the instructions. To press means to bring the iron straight down and lift it to move to the next section. Gliding the iron across the fabric can cause stretching, especially with bias seams as on the triangles in this project.

CARAMEL APPLE PIE

Does anything smell better than a fresh apple pie, laced with cinnamon and nutmeg, baking in the oven? If America had a national dessert, it would probably be apple pie. This recipe is just a little different because it has a subtle caramel flavor, enough to taste, but not to overpower the apples and spices.

Ingredients

Pastry for 9" double crust pie

6 cups thinly sliced apples

Juice from ½ lemon

½ cup packed light brown sugar

½ cup + 1 tablespoon white sugar

2 teaspoons ground cinnamon

¼ teaspoon nutmeg

4 tablespoons flour

¼ cup butter, chilled and diced

12 caramel candy squares, quartered

Directions

1. Preheat over to 375° F (190° C).

2. Toss the apple slices with the lemon juice in a large bowl. Mix the brown sugar, ½ cup white sugar, spices, flour, butter and caramels and stir into the fruit.

3. Roll half of the pastry out and place it inside the pie pan for the bottom crust. Spoon the filling into the crust.

4. Roll out the remaining pastry, cut vent holes and cover the filling. Crimp the top and bottom edges together. Sprinkle lightly with 1 tablespoon sugar.

5. Bake for about 50 minutes until filling is beginning to bubble and crust is golden.

If the filling leaks and makes a mess in the oven, it may be because you forgot to cut steam vents in the top crust. As the fruit cooks, it releases steam and if it has no place to go it will force holes in the sides of the crust and leak juice. And sometimes brushing a glaze of beaten egg over the cut vents can actually seal the vents, causing the same unfortunate results. To avoid these problems, be sure and have adequate vents cut and place the pan on a foil-lined baking sheet to bake. If it leaks, the mess will be easy to clean up.

ANTIQUE APPLE PARER

There are so many old apple parers and so many people that like to collect them, that there is an International Society for Apple Parer Enthusiasts. They have a newsletter and conferences, so apparently there is a great deal of information to be learned about this handy tool.

Apples have long been a staple part of the diet, so it was natural that someone would set out to invent a mechanical device that would make peeling a bushel of apples quick and (relatively) easy. There were almost as many model of apple parers — manufactured and homemade — as there are varieties of apples; and they varied greatly in appearance, though the basic process remained the same. Most were made of wood or iron or a combination, and would turn the apple while an attached blade cut off the peel. Some went a step farther and cored and sliced the fruit. At least one model had a leather strap so the device could be strapped to the leg!

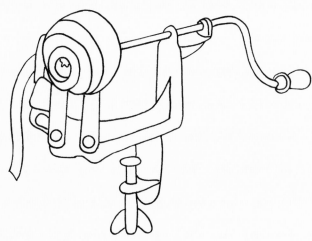

Lemon

We use lemons to flavor our beverages, poultry, fish, vegetables and desserts — what a versatile fruit! If that isn't impressive enough, the ladies of Louis XIV's court used lemons to redden their lips, kings used lemons to astonish others with their wealth and sailors used them (squeezed into a good-size shot of rum) to combat scurvy.

Archaeological evidence shows that lemons probably originated in the Indus Valley — a lemon-shaped earring found there dating from 2500 B.C. seems to prove the point. The fruit became popular in the late Middle Ages, with Crusaders returning from Palestine with this rare and expensive fruit. Lemons have been cultivated on a large scale in the United States since the Gold Rush of 1849 and now California produces one-third of the world's lemons.

Nothing compares to fresh lemons and this pie recipe owes its tangy flavor to the freshly squeezed juice and grated peel. The window valance and apron are sewn with an equally fresh color palette of bright yellow and green prints. The valance hangs from fabric ties and the apron has an old-fashioned gathered skirt with ties and a handy pocket.

WINDOW VALANCE WITH TIES

FINISHED SIZE: 12" x 65" PANEL

A valance is more of a window dressing than a covering and so it can be more fun than practical! The fabric ties on this valance are an interesting detail and quite easy to make. I have included instructions to add a lining, but if sun exposure is not a problem, the lining can be eliminated.

Materials

Fabric:

¾ yd. yellow print

½ yd. green print

13½" x 66" piece of weather-blocking curtain lining (piece if necessary)

Additional Supplies:

Matching sewing threads

Cutting Instructions

From the yellow print, cut
- (1) 12½" x 66" panel (piece as necessary; see Sewing Tips)

From the green print, cut
- (1) 4" x 66" band (piece as necessary; see Sewing Tips)
- (24) 3½" x 12" strips

Instructions

Note: All seams for the valance are ½".

1. Sew the green band to one long edge of the yellow valance. Press the seam toward the green band. This will become the top edge.

2. For the ties, fold each strip in half lengthwise, right sides together. Sew long edges and across one short end. Clip the corners and turn right-side out through the open end. Press well. Repeat to make a total of 24 ties.

3. Place the valance right side up on your work surface. Pin one pair of ties at each end, ¾" from the corner. Evenly space the remaining tie pairs along the top and machine baste in place.

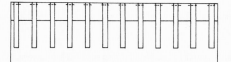

4. Press a 1" hem along one long edge of the lining. Fold the hem up again to make a doubled hem and stitch in place.

5. Pin the lining to the valance with right sides together. Sew the side and top seams. Trim the corners and grade the tie ends in the seam by trimming them to different widths. Turn the valance right side out and press well.

6. Press in the remaining section of the valance sides ½". Press the bottom hem by turning up ½" along the bottom edge and then turning again another 2½". Sew the hem in place, keeping the lining hanging free.

7. Tie each set of ties in a knot over the curtain rod to hang the valance.

RETRO KITCHEN APRON

FINISHED SIZE: 18" x 21"

Aprons are staging a comeback and this "retro" version fits the bill. It has a gathered skirt with a contrasting fabric waistband and ties and bright red buttons to dress it up.

Materials

Fabric:

¾ yd. yellow print

½ yd. green print

Additional Supplies:

Matching sewing threads

12 red buttons, ⅝" diameter

Cutting Instructions

From the yellow print, cut
- (1) 42" x 22" panel for skirt
- (1) 6" x 5" rectangle for pocket

From green print, cut
- (1) 19" x 4½" strip for waistband
- (2) 5½" x 30" strips for ties
- (1) 3¾" x 6" strip for pocket band

Instructions

Note: All seams are ½".

1. Press a ½" hem along both 22" sides of the yellow skirt panel. Fold and press again for a doubled hem and sew in place.

2. Press a ½" hem along one long edge. Fold and press another 2" for the bottom hem and sew in place.

3. Adjust the stitch length to a gathering stitch and sew two lines of stitching ½" and ¼" from the top edge of the skirt. Leave the threads free at both ends.

4. Draw the bobbin threads from both ends until the gathered skirt measures 18" across. Tie the threads together to stabilize the size and adjust the gathers until they are evenly spaced.

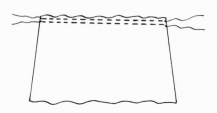

5. Sew the gathered end of the skirt to one long side of the waistband, right sides together, leaving a ½" margin on each end of the waistband.

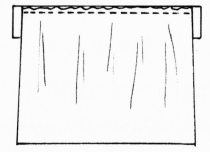

6. Press a ½" hem on the other long side of the waistband.

7. Fold each green tie in half lengthwise, right sides together, and sew down the long edges and across one short end. Trim the corners and turn right side out through the open end. Press well.

8. Fold a ¼" pleat on each raw end and baste to hold. (The tie width should now measure 1¾" across.

9. Baste the raw ends of the ties to the ends of the waistband.

10. Fold the waistband in half lengthwise, right sides together, and sew the end seams even with the side hems as seen below. Trim the corners and turn right side out.

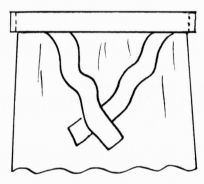

11. Slipstitch the folded edge of the waistband to the inside.

12. Refer to the Pocket directions on page 132 in the Techniques chapter for details and photos to prepare the apron pocket.

13. Sew the green band to the yellow pocket along one 6" side.

14. Sew a ¼" hem on the other 6" side of the green band.

15. Fold the band over to the inside of the pocket and sew a seam on each side. Trim the seam.

16. Turn the band right side out and press in the ½" seam allowance on the sides and bottom of the pocket. To miter the bottom corners, first fold up the corner diagonally, trim the excess fabric and then fold the adjacent sides in. Slipstitch the miter folds to hold them in place.

17. Baste the pocket to the apron about 3¾" down from the waistband and 4¼" in from the side. (Place the pocket on whichever side you prefer.) Sew close to the edge on the pocket sides and bottom.

18. Sew three buttons to the pocket band.

19. Sew nine buttons evenly spaced across the front of the waistband

Whenever you are piecing several layers that will be sewn together as one, such as the valance, band and lining, stagger the seams so they don't all fall together, forming a bulky spot.

When you have a lot of small pieces to sew, such as the ties for the valance, chain piecing (or assembly-line piecing), is a good way to get the job done. Sew the first seam and instead of removing those pieces from under the presser foot and clipping the thread, just leave them in place. Slip the next set of pieces under the foot, right next to the set you have just sewn, and continue sewing. This technique saves time and thread and it eliminates the annoying habit the machine has of eating the beginning stitches of a seam. When you are all finished, clip the threads between each set.

As a general rule, the width of a valance should be about 2 to 2½ times the width of the window for fullness.

If you are using a rotary cutting system and have trouble with the ruler slipping as you cut, try attaching sandpaper dots or masking tape to the underside of your ruler. Standing, rather than sitting, also helps by giving you better control.

LEMON SOUR CREAM PIE

Although this pie would taste good anytime of year, summer seems the best time to enjoy anything lemon-y. From a lemon wedge in a glass of ice water, a pitcher of lemonade or this tangy pie, the tartness of lemon seems to offer a relief from the heat.

Ingredients

Baked and cooled 9" pastry shell

1 cup plus 6 tablespoons sugar

¼ cup cornstarch

Dash of salt

1 cup milk

3 eggs, separated

¼ cup butter

½ teaspoon grated lemon peel

¼ cup fresh lemon juice

1 cup dairy sour cream

¼ teaspoon cream of tartar

½ teaspoon vanilla

Directions

1. Preheat the oven to 350° F (175° C).

2. Combine 1 cup of the sugar with the cornstarch and salt in a saucepan, stirring thoroughly.

3. Slowly stir in the milk, then cook and stir over medium heat until the mixture is boiling and thickened.

4. Remove the pan from the heat. Blend a small amount of hot mixture into the slightly beaten egg yolks. Return the egg yolk mixture to the hot mixture in the pan; cook and stir 2 minutes over medium heat.

5. Add butter, lemon peel and lemon juice. Cover and cool.

6. Fold in the sour cream and spoon the mixture into the baked pie shell.

7. Beat the egg whites with cream of tartar and vanilla until soft peaks form. Gradually add the remaining 6 tablespoons of sugar, beating until stiff peaks form. Top the pie with meringue, sealing to the edges of the pastry.

8. Bake in preheated oven for 12-15 minutes or until meringue is golden. Cool. Store in the refrigerator.

When baking an unfilled pie shell, there are several things that you can do to prevent shrinkage or puffy spots. Never pull or stretch the dough when fitting it into a pan. Use a fork to generously prick the dough before baking to allow the steam to escape without pushing the crust up. Lastly, line the crust with foil and place purchased pie weights or dry beans or rice in the bottom. Bake for about half the time and remove the foil and weights. Return the pastry to the oven and finish baking.

ANTIQUE LEMON SQUEEZER

Made from wood, heavy cast aluminum, iron, glass or porcelain, lemon squeezers were designed to free the housewife of having to squeeze the lemons with her hands. Some were tabletop models, some had compartments to catch the seeds and the really fancy ones could also perform other tasks such as cracking nuts and pressing garlic cloves. Instructions usually encouraged the cook to roll the lemon on the table first to produce the most juice.

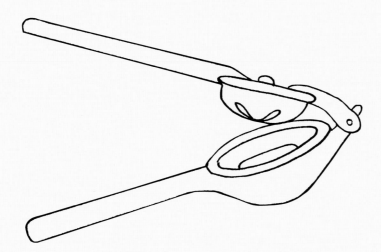

Strawberry

Strawberries are one of the most popular of summer fruits — strawberry stands and U-Pick signs dot the countryside when the sweet berries are ripening. Most berries though are not sold fresh at the market, but are processed into sliced or whole frozen berries or pureed for other uses. Strawberries retain most of their sweetness in all their processed forms so we can enjoy them all year round. But nothing beats a shortcake or pie piled high with freshly picked strawberries — even a simple bowl of berries is a treat.

Strawberries have a history that goes back over 2200 years. Strawberries grew wild in Italy as early as 234 B.C. Wild strawberries were discovered in Virginia when ships landed there in 1588. Early settlers cultivated their own berries, as did the Native Americans. Some believe the name "strawberry" came from the practice of scattering straw around the growing plants to protect the tender vines from harsh weather. Others say, it derived from the Anglo-Saxon "to strew" (spread) in relationship to the plant's runners.

A fresh strawberry pie with glazed sweet berries and whipped cream is as beautiful as it is delicious.

A pot of tea to accompany that pie could be kept hot and ready to serve inside this strawberry tea cozy. The appliqués are fused and finished with embroidery and little black buttons to represent the seeds. The matching coasters make it a special set.

TEA COZY WITH STRAWBERRY APPLIQUÉS

FINISHED SIZE: 13½" x 11"

A fanciful vine of strawberries is embroidered and appliquéd onto the front of this padded and lined tea cozy. Self-made piping and bias tape to match the fabrics trim the edges.

Materials

Fabric:

1 yd. tan mini check (for cozy and lining)

Fat quarter green mini dot

Scrap of red print

Additional Supplies:

Batting

Matching sewing threads

Green embroidery floss

Black embroidery floss

9 black buttons, ¼" diameter

1 yd. cable (piping) cord, ⅛" diameter

14" x 11" sheet of paper for pattern (newspaper sheet will work)

Standard size dinner plate for pattern

Iron-on adhesive

Embroidery needle

Air soluble pen

Zipper foot for sewing machine

Patterns (page 138-139):

Vine

Strawberry

Strawberry Cap

Leaf

Cutting Instructions

From the tan check, cut
(4) cozy pieces (See Step 1-2)

From the green dot, cut
- 1¼"-wide bias strips (enough to piece to make 36" length)
- 1⅛"-wide bias strips (enough to piece to make 30" length)

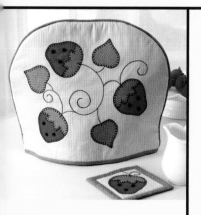

Instructions

1. To make a pattern for the tea cozy, fold the paper in half so it measures 7" x 11". Place the dinner plate at the top edge of the paper and trace only the curve of the plate onto the paper on the unfolded corners.

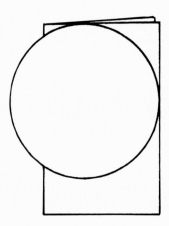

2. Cut out the pattern and use it to cut out four cozy pieces (front, back and lining) from the tan fabric and two from the batting.

3. Use the air soluble pen to transfer the vine pattern to the center of one cozy piece (front).

4. Use two strands of green embroidery floss to sew an outline stitch along the pattern lines.

5. Trace the strawberry, cap and leaf patterns three times each onto the paper side of the iron-on adhesive, leaving a ½" margin between the shapes.

6. Cut the shapes apart, leaving a small margin around the traced lines.

7. Place the strawberry shapes on the wrong side of the red print and the strawberry caps and leaves on the wrong side of the green dot. Refer to the manufacturer's directions for iron setting and time to transfer the adhesive to the fabric.

8. Cut out the appliqués on the traced lines, cutting through the paper and fabric. Remove the paper backing.

9. Refer to the photo and place a strawberry with a cap on top at the end of each appropriate stem. Place the leaves at the end of the other stems. Fuse the appliqués in place.

10. Use two strands of black embroidery floss to blanket stitch around each appliqué.

11. Sandwich one piece of batting between the cozy front and a lining piece with the wrong sides together and machine or hand baste all around, about ¾₆" from the edge. Repeat with the cozy back.

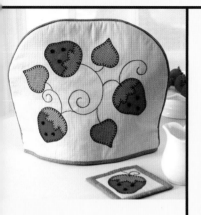

12. Sew three black buttons to each strawberry as shown in the photo and pattern, sewing through all layers.

13. Refer to Piping on page 130 in the Technique chapter for details and photos to make the piping trim. Do not gather fabric on cording. Wrap the 1¼"-wide fabric strips around the cord and sew close to the cord using a zipper foot on the machine. Trim the flat side of the piping to ¼".

14. Pin the piping around the sides and top of the cozy front, with the raw edge of the piping even with the raw edge of the cozy. With the zipper foot still attached, machine baste close to the cord. Trim away any excess cord.

15. Pin the cozy front and back right sides together and sew the sides and top.

16. Finish the seam by machine sewing a close zig zag stitch, serging the edges or hand sewing a small blanket stitch to cover the raw edges.

17. Carefully press a ¼" hem along one long side of the 1⅛"-wide bias strip and one short end.

18. Starting with the folded end at the back of the cozy, pin the raw edge of the bias strip around the bottom edge of the cozy, right sides together. Overlap the ends ½", trimming any excess. Stitch in place.

19. Fold the tape over the bottom edge of the cozy and hand sew the folded edge to the inside.

STRAWBERRY COASTERS

FINISHED SIZE: 4½" x 4½"

Using the same strawberry motif as on the cozy, each coaster is bordered and quilted near the edge. Stacked and tied with ribbon, these would make a lovely gift.

Materials (for one)

Fabric:

Scraps of tan mini check, green dot and red print

Additional Supplies:

5" x 5" batting

Matching sewing threads

Green embroidery floss

Black embroidery floss

3 black buttons, ¼" diameter

Iron-on adhesive

Air soluble pen

Patterns (page 139):

Stem

Strawberry

Strawberry Cap

Cutting Instructions

From the tan check, cut
• (1) 4" x 4" square

From the green dot, cut
• (2) 1" x 4" strips
• (2) 1" x 5" strips
• (1) 5" x 5" square

Instructions

1. Prepare a strawberry and strawberry cap appliqué following Steps 5-8 in the Tea Cozy instructions.

2. Refer to the photo and place the strawberry at an angle on the tan square. Position the cap on top and fuse in place.

3. Use two strands of black floss to blanket stitch around the appliqués.

4. Transfer the stem pattern to the top of the berry with an air soluble pen.

5. Outline stitch on the stem lines with two strands of green floss.

6. Sew the 4" strips to the sides of the strawberry square; press the seams outward.

7. Sew the 5" strips to the top and bottom of the strawberry square; press the seams outward.

8. Place the 5" fabric square on top of the batting, right side up; place the appliquéd square right side down and pin the layers together. Sew all around, leaving a 3" opening along one side. Trim the batting close to the seam, trim the corners and turn right side out. Press well.

9. Fold in the seam allowance on the opening and hand sew the opening closed with a small whipstitch from edge to edge.

10. Hand or machine quilt by stitching close to the seam line around the borders.

11. Sew the black buttons to the strawberry, where indicated on the pattern, sewing through all layers.

Iron-on adhesive has made appliqué so easy and quick, but you have to plan ahead to place each piece before applying the iron. If you need to remove a fused appliqué, however, it is possible. Set the iron at the same setting as for fusing and hold it on the piece for about the same amount of time. Before it begins to cool, lift up a corner and peel the appliqué off. A pin is helpful to lift it off at the corner. Some residue may be left but the new appliqué piece should cover it.

GLAZED FRESH STRAWBERRY PIE

The glaze for this pie has an extra ingredient — strawberry flavored gelatin — which adds body and even more flavor to the filling. The fresher and sweeter the berries, the better the pie!

Ingredients

9" deep-dish or regular 10" pie shell, baked and cooled

1 cup sugar

¼ cup cornstarch

Dash of salt

1 pkg. (3 oz.) strawberry gelatin

1 qt. fresh strawberries, cleaned, sliced or halved and well-drained

Whipped cream for garnish

Directions

1. In a medium saucepan, combine the sugar, cornstarch and salt. Stir in the water and bring to a boil over medium-high heat. Boil one minute; mixture should be slightly thickened and clear.

2. Add the gelatin and stir until dissolved. Cool to room temperature.

3. Stir the strawberries into the gelatin mixture. Turn into pie shell and chill 4-6 hours or until set. Serve topped with whipped cream, if desired.

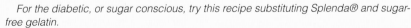

For the diabetic, or sugar conscious, try this recipe substituting Splenda® and sugar-free gelatin.

For a really yummy alternative, combine 3 oz. soft cream cheese with 1 tablespoon of light cream. Spread on the bottom of the cooled pie shell before adding the strawberries.

ANTIQUE STRAWBERRY HULLER

A strawberry huller, which also promised to double as a pin-feather puller, worked like a wide pair of tweezers to pick the strawberry cap off the berry. According to the advertisement for the "Nip-It" huller, by its use "one avoids stained fingers, seeds under fingernails and crushed fruit." They were inexpensive, small and light and very simple to use — very practical, even today!

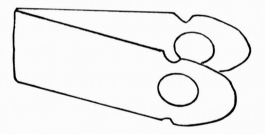

Techniques

In this section you will find some techniques or steps that are used in a number of the projects, so I am showing them here as a reference. Also I included some steps that I felt could use a visual to help better communicate the process.

YO-YO FLOWERS

Yo-Yo flowers are formed from fabric circles that are hemmed and gathered into small rosettes. They can be sewn together to make a bedcover, pillow front or vest or used individually as an embellishment. Yo-Yo quilts were popular in the 1930s usually made from a wide variety of scraps. Now they are most often used to decorate wearables and home projects.

1. Finger press a small (about ¾₆") hem as you sew gathering stitches all around the fabric circle.

2. Pull the gathers up rightly and push the hole to the center.

3. One way to finish the Yo-Yo flower is to place a fabric-covered shank button over the hole.

PADDED APPLIQUÉS

Sometimes I use fleece to pad my appliqués to give dimensional interest to the project. This method gives a smooth, accurate outer edge to the shapes.

1. Stack the two layers of fabric, right sides together with the pattern on top, onto the fleece and sew all around on the pattern lines.

2. Cut out the shape and trim the fleece close to the seam. Using small sharp scissors, make a slash through one layer of the fabric only.

3. Turn the shape right side out through the slash and press well.

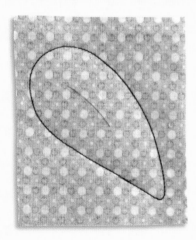

PIPING

Piping accents the edges of some of my sewing projects. You can buy it ready-made or follow these steps to make custom piping to coordinate beautifully with your own fabrics. Bias fabric strips are used whenever the piped edges are curved.

1. When it is necessary to join strips to obtain the needed length, use a diagonal seam to eliminate bulk. Pin the ends together at right angles and sew across diagonally. Trim the seam to ¼" and press the seam open.

2. When the seam is sewn in this manner, it distributes the bulk and makes the seam almost invisible.

3. Wrap the fabric strip around the cable cord and sew very close to the cord using a zipper foot. The piping can be finished flat or shirred.

4. You may gather fabric on the piping for extra dimension.

ADDING TRIANGLES TO SQUARES

This method is more accurately described as adding squares to squares and then trimming to make triangles within squares, but that is way too long of a title! By using squares you can eliminate the need to cut and work with triangles which can be tricky because of the bias edge.

1. Draw a diagonal line from one corner to the opposing corner on the small fabric square and pin this to the large square as shown.

2. Sew a seam on the drawn line.

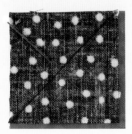

3. Trim seam to ¼".

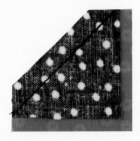

4. Fold triangle back and press.

POCKETS

This is a simple method to make an unlined patch pocket with a contrasting band, as on the apron skirt in the Lemon chapter.

1. Hem the contrasting band on one side and stitch the opposing side to the top of the pocket piece.

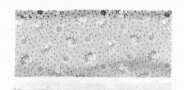

2. Fold the band over with the right sides together and stitch the side seams. Trim the seam.

3. Fold the band over into the inside and press the sides and bottom seam allowances to the inside. Fold and press a miter on the two lower corners. Tack the miter in place with a few hand stitches.

4. Sew the prepared pocket to the front of the apron by topstitching close to the edge.

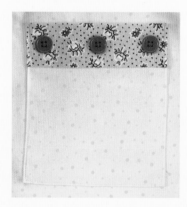

EMBROIDERY STITCHES

The embroidery stitches I have used in this book are very common and quite simple but add a lot to a project. The blanket stitch is used primarily around the edges of appliqués or to finish the edge of a cloth. The outline stitch is used for any line or outline of shapes.

1. Blanket Stitch

2. Outline Stitch

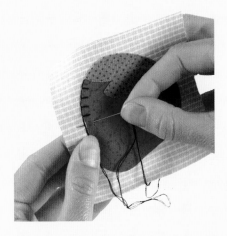

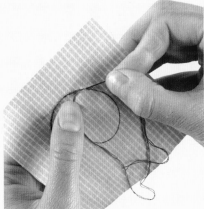

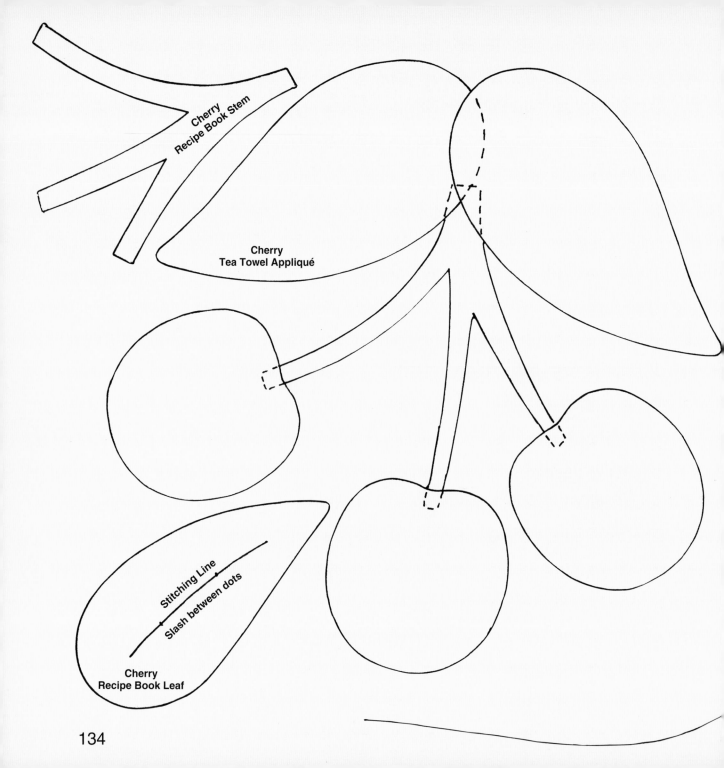

Cherry
Recipe Book Stem

Cherry
Tea Towel Appliqué

Stitching Line

Slash between dots

Cherry
Recipe Book Leaf

134

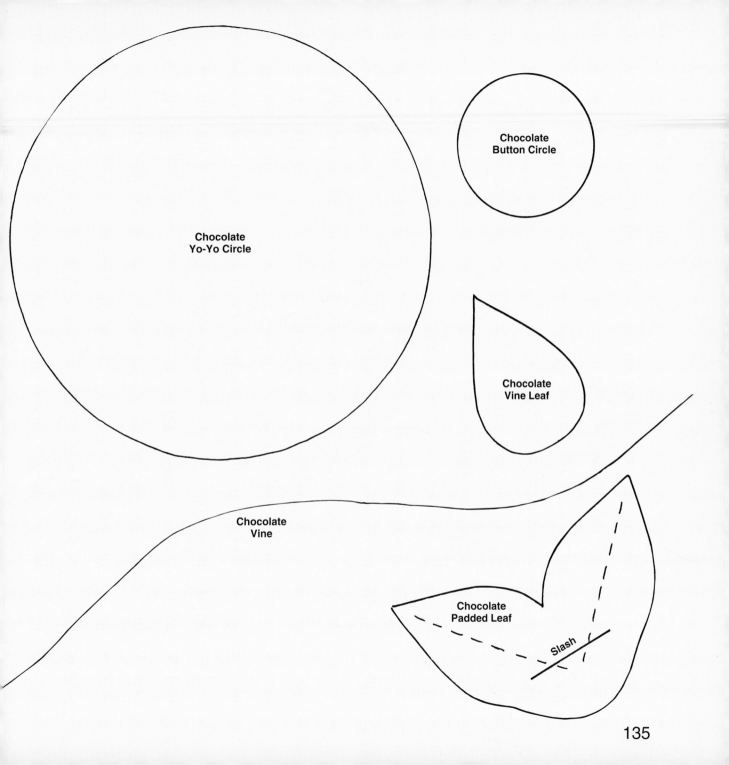

Chocolate
Yo-Yo Circle

Chocolate
Button Circle

Chocolate
Vine Leaf

Chocolate
Vine

Chocolate
Padded Leaf

Slash

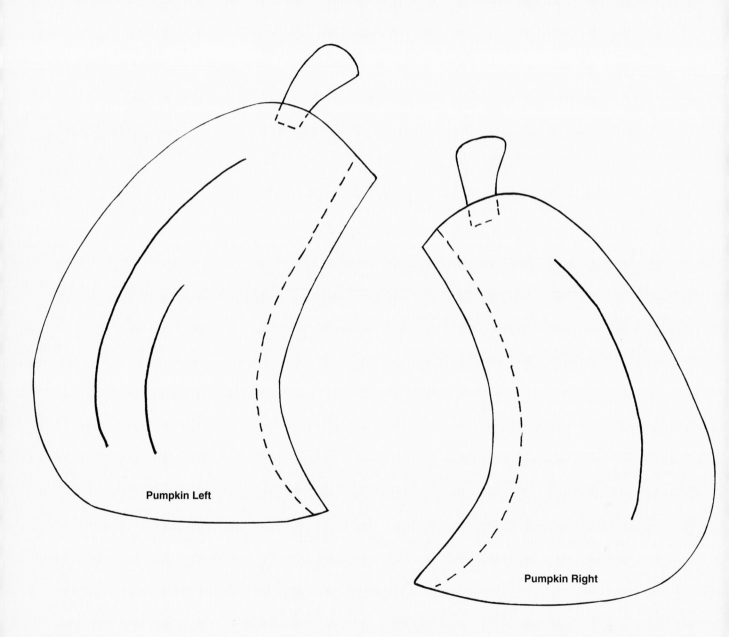

Pumpkin Left

Pumpkin Right

136

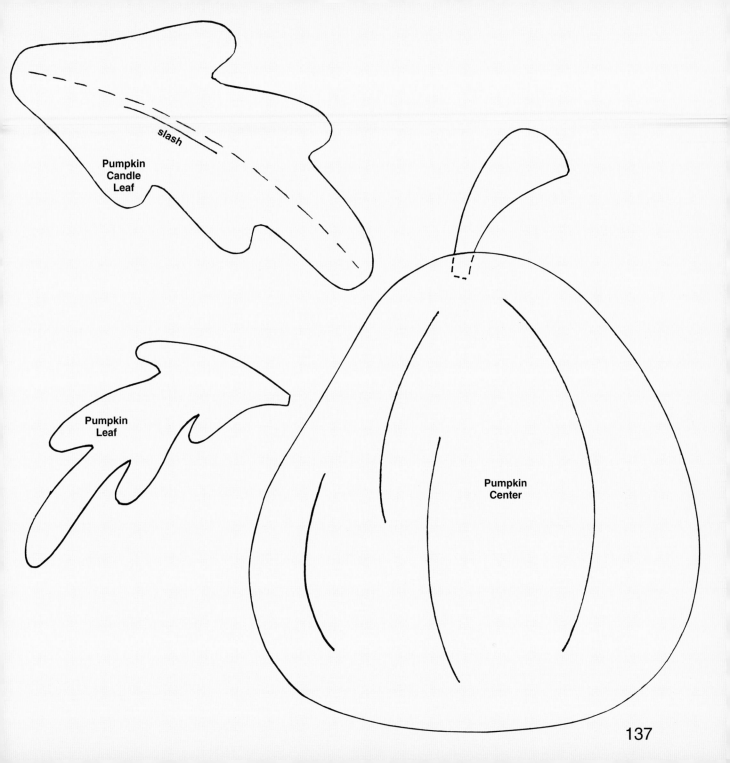

Pumpkin
Candle
Leaf

slash

Pumpkin
Leaf

Pumpkin
Center

137

Strawberry
Vine

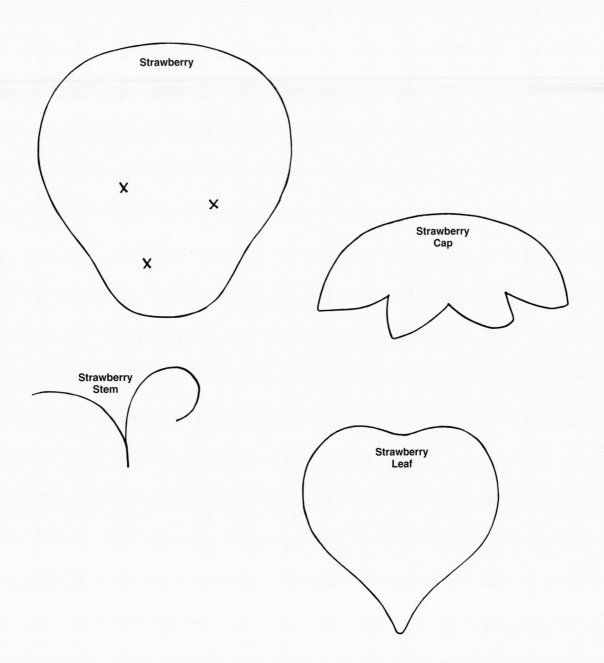

Strawberry

Strawberry
Cap

Strawberry
Stem

Strawberry
Leaf

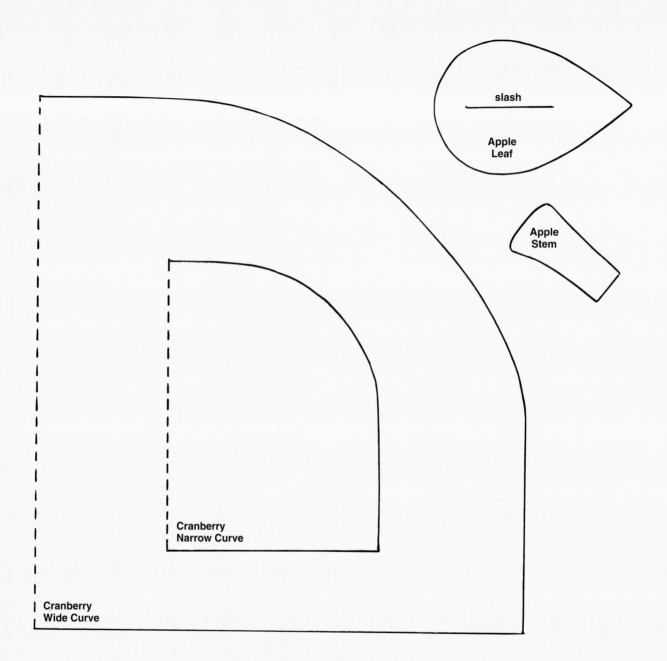

slash

Apple Leaf

Apple Stem

Cranberry Narrow Curve

Cranberry Wide Curve

140

Resources

Sewing Supplies

Beacon Adhesives, Inc.
125 MacQuesten Parkway S.
Mt. Vernon, NY 10550
(800) 865-7238
www.beaconcreates.com
Fabri-Tac™ Permanent Adhesive

Clover Needlecraft, Inc.
13438 Alondra Blvd.
Cerritos, CA 90703
(562) 282-0200
www.clover-usa.com
Bags & Totes Handles #6324

DMC ® Corp.
S. Hackensack Ave.
Port Kearny Building
South Kearny, NJ 07032
www.dmc-usa.com
*Embroidery floss, pearl cotton,
quilting thread*

Dunroven House
P.O. Box 3070
Mooresville, NC 28117
(704) 896-8904
www.dunrovenhouse.com
Tea towels

Fairfield Processing Corp.
P.O. Box 1157
Danbury, CT 06813
(203) 744-2090
www.poly-fil.com
Soft n Crafty ® Premium Pillow Form

Freudenberg Nonwovens
3440 Industrial Drive
www.freudenberg-nw.com
Durham, NC 27704
Pellon ® Fusible Fleece

Prym Consumer USA Inc.
P.O. Box 5028
Spartanburg, SC 29304
(864)576-5050
www.dritz.com
Fray Check
Cover Button Kit
Sew-On Hook and Eye Closures

The Warm™ Company
954 E. Union St.
Seattle, WA 98122
(800) 324-WARM
www.warmcompany.com
*Soft & Bright ™ Needled
Polyester Batting*
*Warm & Bright ™ Needled
Cotton Batting*
*Insul-Bright ™ Insulated
Needlepunched Lining*

Therm O Web
770 Glenn Ave.
Wheeling, IL 60090
(800) 323-0799
www.thermoweb.com
*HeatnBond ® Iron-On Adhesive: Lite,
Ultra Hold*

Wrights ®
West Warren, MA 01092
(877) 597-4448
www.wrights.com
Rick Rack
Cable Cord
Simply Creative ™ Seed Bead Wire

Books

Franklin, Linda Campbell. ***From
Hearth to Cookstove.*** USA: House
of Collectibles, Inc., 1978.
Franklin, Linda Campbell. ***300 Years
of Kitchen Collectibles.*** USA:
Krause Publications, 1997
The Wise Encyclopedia of Cookery.
USA: Wm. H. Wise & Co., Inc., 1948

About the Author

Chris Malone has been sewing and crafting most of her life and has been a professional designer for many years. She has had hundreds of designs published in industry magazines. She is also the author of **Kitchen Stitchin'** (KP Books 2005) and **Sew It in Minutes** (KP Books 2006) as well as several booklets and has contributed to many multi-artist books. She owned a restaurant and an antique store with her husband for many years. She resides on the beautiful southern Oregon coast.

More Savvy Stitching Tips and Techniques

Sip 'n Sew
by Diane Dhein

Simple-to-sew gifts, smart stitching techniques and sassy spirits to boot! There's not much left out of this exciting new sewing and spirit serving combo guide. Inside you'll find instructions for 20 stitched gifts, and related drink recipes, such as Mandarin Spice Tea and Asian tea party mats.

Softcover
8 x 8 • 160 pages
75 color illus.
Item# Z0981 • $19.99

Stitch Spritz & Sew
Curved Piecing as Easy as 1-2-3
by Kathy Bowers

Pick up a quick and simple appliqué method for stitching on a curve, curved piecing that is. Create mirror image frames, and arcs all while learning how to add new design elements to basic quilting.

Softcover
8¼ x 10⅞ • 128 pages
60 color photos
Item# Z1311 • $22.99

Sew It In Minutes
24 Projects to Fit Your Style and Schedule
by Chris Malone

Discover how to create each of the 24 projects in this book in 60, 90, 120, 240 minutes or less. Projects include ornaments, photo frames, appliquéd bibs and more.

Softcover
8¼ x 10⅞ • 128 pages
175 color photos and illus.
Item# Z0133 • $22.99

Kitchen Stitchin'
50 Quick and Easy Projects to Liven Up your Table
by Chris Malone

Quickly and easily create 50 distinctive pieces for kitchens and dining areas using quilting, embroidery, sewing, rug hooking, appliqué, beading and other techniques! This guide includes instructions for place mats, recipe album, toaster covers, napkins, wine bag, coasters and more.

Softcover
8¼ x 10⅞ • 128 pages
175+ color photos
Item# KTBLD • $21.99

Claire Shaeffer's Fabric Sewing Guide
2nd Edition
by Claire Shaeffer

This full-color edition of the ultimate one-stop sewing resource is great for new and savvy sewers alike, with easy-to-read charts for needle sizes, and thread and stabilizer types.

Softcover
8¼ x 10⅞ • 504 pages
75 b&w illus.
225 color photos
Item# Z0933 • $39.99